orange

A BOOK OF INSTRUCTIONS

by chloe park

dear yoko,
thank you for showing me the power of Light.

dear john,
thank you for being my first teacher.

dear halmoni, komo #1, komo #2, komobu,
thank you for believing in me & your
unconditional love and support.

hi friend!

thank you for pickin' up my book!
i wrote this when i was living
in mexico in 2011.

this is my humble offering to you,
in hopes to ignite light. may you walk
your path with joy and courage.
may we all wake up together.

hari om, i love you,
chlo X

TO DO LISTS!

part one

1. close your eyes
2. inhale
3. exhale
4. feel

1. take off your shoes
2. open your front door
3. walk to your favorite tree
4. count the steps

1. lay down on your back
2. place your left palm
   on your heart
3. feel the beat

1. lay on your back
2. place your right hand
   on your belly
3. feel your breath travel

1. write down a list of what
   you are grateful for

1. write down a list
   of your fears
2. go to the ocean
3. burn the list

1. go to the ocean
   on a full moon
2. take off all
   your clothes
3. go swimming

1. grow your hair for peace

1. love everyone
2. tell the truth
3. be open, always

1. give love
2. receive love
3. repeat

1. look in the mirror
2. smile

1. write down every emotion
   you've experienced today
2. read it tomorrow

1. keep a pen & paper
   with you, always
2. write down ideas,
   thoughts, songs, etc

1. look up
2. count the clouds

1. look forward
2. count the trees

1. massage your feet -
   they take you everywhere

QUESTIONS OF
INQUIRY
to: Self

part two

what are you naturally good at?
what comes easily for you?

whose footsteps do you admire?

1._____
2._____
3._____

why?

what are the top 5 topics
roaming around your brain?

1._____
2._____
3._____
4._____
5._____

where do you feel the most peace?

what was the first song
you heard that changed your life?

what are some books you've read
that have expanded the intelligence
of your mind?

who are some artists, painters, musicians,
poets, writers, sculptors, photographers,
etc - whose work moves you?

who are you listening to at the moment?

what do you say to yourself
when you first awake?

what are some of your favorite memories?

what qualities of your
Self do you most admire?

what qualities of your
Self would you like to change?

what are your goals, dreams,
visions, and aspirations?

who are the closest people
to you in your life?

what are the dynamics like?

you

who is rotating around you
at this moment?

who is the closest?

who is the furthest?

what are some of the most current
lessons that you've learnt?

what are some of your
biggest challenges?

1._____
2._____
3._____
4._____
5._____

in order of presence, please place accordingly.
(in regards to your life *at this moment.*)

career, Self, family, friends,
lover, puppy, (__insert here__)

1._____
2._____
3._____
4._____
5._____
6._____
7._____

who do you hold in your heart?

1._____

2._____

3._____

4._____

5._____

how do you show and express love?

what makes you feel loved?

what are some of your private rituals?

who knows you

?

what relationships in your
life do you most treasure?

GAMES &
EXPERIMENTS

part three

imagine you live underwater.

how would you move?
how would you breathe?
what kind of creature
would you be?

when interacting with another human,
imagine you are a mute.

don't talk for an entire day.
receive everything.

find a comfortable seat.
set your alarm for one hour.
close your eyes, sit down,
and breathe.

count how many steps
you walk in one day.

do everything with
your opposite hand.

carry fresh rosemary with
you at all times.

inhale & smell
when necessary.

smile all day long.

laugh at everything anyone says,
even if it's not funny.

feel the breeze and say thank you,
close your eyes and say i love you.

sprinkle a little more love
onto every single thing you do.

Chloe Park - Artist, Healer, Spiritual Teacher,
Writer and Ethnobotanist. She roams the Earth
to share her message of healing, love and truth.
Deeply influenced by the lives and works of
Gandhi, Yoko Ono, John Lennon & Mother Theresa,
she is a devotee to the awakening process
of all sentient beings and to the recovery
of the human soul and spirit.

Her work is inspired by
nature, freedom and beauty.

www.chloeparkhealing.com

Cover artwork by Luckey Remington

may all beings find inner peace

blessings ॐ

www.ingramcontent.com/pod-product-compliance
Lightning Source LLC
LaVergne TN
LVHW021118080426
835509LV00021B/3442